# Planning High School Courses

## Charting the Course toward Homeschool Graduation

# Lee Binz,
## The HomeScholar

First Printing, 2018

Printed in the United States of America
Cover Design by Robin Montoya
Edited by Kimberly Charron

ISBN: 1511558423
ISBN-13: 978-1511558426

# Planning High School Courses

Charting the Course toward
Homeschool Graduation

# What are
# Coffee Break Books?

*Planning High School Courses* is part of The HomeScholar's Coffee Break Book series.

Designed especially for parents who don't want to spend hours and hours reading a 400-page book on homeschooling high school, each book combines Lee's practical and friendly approach with detailed, but easy-to-digest information, perfect to read over a cup of coffee at your favorite coffee shop!

Never overwhelming, always accessible and manageable, each book in the series will give parents the tools they need to tackle the tasks of homeschooling high school, one warm sip at a time.

Everything about these Coffee Break Books is designed to connote simplicity, ease and comfort - from the size (fits in a purse), to the font and paragraph length (easy on the eyes), to the price (the same as a Starbucks Venti Triple Caramel Macchiato). Unlike a fancy coffee drink, however, these books are guilt-free pleasures you will want to enjoy again and again!

# Table of Contents

Introduction

# "Real World" Homeschoolers

There are two kinds of parents who consider homeschooling high school. Some parents ooze confidence with super-human academic and organizational capability. They often have near-perfect children, compliant in every situation. They have plenty of time to digest detailed information about high school. They thrive on research, and enjoy learning the nuances of senior year before their children become teenagers. If you are reading this book, you are most likely not one of these parents!

My biggest fans, however, are parents who live in "the real world" with real stress. They can be slightly terrified sometimes or even occasionally freaked out, and they often feel a little overwhelmed by all the details of homeschooling high school. I have met these parents at conventions. I know you are out there! But I also know how much you love your children and want to do a good job. If you're one of these parents, I want to offer you support as you plan high school courses. In this book, we'll discuss college prep requirements for each high school subject area and learn strategies for choosing and teaching some of the harder subjects.

There are two questions I often hear from parents who are planning to homeschool high school. The first one is, "How do I get them to do the work?" Unfortunately, children are free moral agents who sometimes do not cooperate, but I can give you some general tips.

The first thing is to get your spouse to play the role of the principal. Sometimes, the job of homeschooling can be so overwhelming; it's helpful if you don't mix-up the job of educating your children with the job of giving out consequences. If you can defer giving the consequences to your spouse when you are the primary teacher, it can be helpful.

Another solution is to define clear, natural consequences with a direct "if ... then" statement. "If you do not turn in your math assignment for the day, then you may not leave the house." Just as you did when your children were toddlers, it can be effective to take what is most important to your teen and withhold it for the purposes of making sure they get their schoolwork done. Their computer, cell phone, or whatever it is they truly love and can't live without, is a good thing to use for natural consequences. See Appendix 1 for more on this vexing issue.

The second question that I often hear is, "How do you get them to work independently?" Many people think high school students should be able to teach themselves. The truth is, you don't suddenly wake up on the first day of ninth grade and discover that your child is perfectly willing and capable of working independently.

Instead, it's a training process, and it's much like teaching a baby how to walk. When kids are ready to walk, they don't stand up and walk; you spend a long time hunched over them, following from behind, holding them up, encouraging them, and holding a cookie so they'll want to walk independently. Frankly, they fall down an awful lot. They're not called toddlers for nothing; they toddle and then they fall. Expect your teenagers to try to work independently, and expect them to fail to act independently. Your job is to follow them from behind, pick them up and hold their hands, and guide them. The resources here in the pages to follow will help you do your best job.

Chapter 1

# English

If you're giving your student a college prep education in high school, the English requirement is four years of reading and writing at their level. You can use a pre-measured curriculum such as Right Start or Institute for Excellence in Writing, or you can count the number of hours spent on the subject in a day. Your student should do a combination of reading and writing for at least an hour a day. There are some kids who always have their noses in a book, reading for two hours a day, then writing for half an hour a day, and this still counts as one credit.

An English course can include a huge variety of topics: spelling, grammar, vocabulary, punctuation, penmanship, reading for fun, reading for class, public speaking, reports, poetry, prose, research writing, short reports, and book reports. Combining these topics can result in one English credit. The only time you would award more than one credit is if you use two complete, pre-measured programs or curriculum, which I do not recommend!

I once had a horrible year when my children used Learn to Write the Novel Way at the same time they worked through the Sonlight Literature and Composition program. It was a nightmare to do more than one complete English curriculum at the same time, and it's not something I recommend. Sometimes a child has a passionate interest in English and it is possible for them to do Learn to Write the Novel Way while going through the Institute for Excellence in Writing program. If that's the case, you can give them two credits, but in general, give them one credit.

Be careful not to overwork your child or duplicate subjects. It's not uncommon for parents to say, "My child is struggling in English; I need to get him up to this level," and they pile on the work, using an entire curriculum for everything. If you're supplementing in your child's weak areas, there's a real possibility of overwork, which can sometimes burn out a kid. If you do have a child who is struggling, then sometimes having them work too hard on a particular subject can make it more hated and more difficult to learn; rather than bringing them up to grade level more quickly, it slows down the process.

English is a great opportunity to create a delight directed course (which is something your child learns because they love a subject), such as novel writing. My brother in-law teaches at a public high school, and he taught a class called "Sports Communication." His daughter was in the class, and she said they spent most of their time listening to baseball play-by-plays, because her dad is a big baseball fan.

This shows that any delight directed learning can be turned into a fabulous class; as a homeschooler, you have the option of choosing anything. In a public school, courses are limited by the teachers' interests, but in your homeschool, courses are only limited by your child's interests. Delight directed learning can go anywhere, such as the sonnets of Shakespeare or the works of Jane Austen. What a great homeschool advantage!

Chapter 2

# Math

Your student should take a math course at their level during every year of high school. Colleges want to see math during a student's senior year, and in order to do well on college application tests such as the SAT or the ACT, your student needs to have Algebra 2 before their junior year.

The standard order to go about math courses is to take Pre-Algebra, Algebra 1, Geometry, and Algebra 2. Sometimes, Geometry and Algebra 2 are flipped, Algebra 2 before Geometry. Both Pre-Calculus and Trigonometry are also interchangeable, and Calculus is sometimes added on.

There are several alternatives to these standard courses, such as Discrete or

Applied Math. In the book by Harold Jacobs called *Mathematics in Human Endeavors*, each chapter includes a math concept that's applied to a specific thing, such as physics or chemistry. Other class alternatives include "Statistics," "Business Math," or "Consumer Math." Choose a course based on your child's level.

Sometimes people ask, "Exactly how much math is required, because my child is so far behind?" Don't feel incapable of homeschooling because your child is behind in math. Frankly, many kids in public and private high school are also behind in math. This doesn't mean you can't move forward. If your child isn't in Algebra 1 in ninth grade, keep working at math at your child's level all the time, and don't beat yourself up about it.

The value of math is that it can be a gateway to college and career. Sometimes people are surprised at the different math required for careers. You would assume that an engineering degree would require a lot of math, but people don't often assume that nursing does, too. I'm a registered nurse, and nursing requires a lot of math. Math truly is a gateway to many college majors and different careers. If you have trouble convincing your child that math is important, I would like to point out that I used algebra every single day while I was working as a nurse. If I did my algebra incorrectly, there was the possibility of a life-threatening medication mistake!

Teaching advanced topics can be nerve-racking for some parents. However, everybody loses the ability to teach math at some point. When you feel as if you've run up against the end limit of what you can teach, there are a couple of things you can do to continue to be successful. One is to choose a homeschool curriculum, which assumes neither you nor your student has a clue about what's going on. Try to get a homeschool curriculum that has online or telephone support, so you can call in and get help whenever you need it.

Let your children use the answer key. It's perfectly acceptable for your child to teach themselves, looking at the textbook or answer key, and working through it step by step. When I left my children during their Algebra 2 tests, I took the answer key, put it in the car and went to the grocery store. By the time I got home, the test was done.

There are a variety of homeschool curriculum in DVD format that include online and telephone support. Sometimes the problem with math is not that Mom or Dad doesn't know how to teach it; the problem is that your curriculum isn't a perfect fit for your child, often because the child has specific irritations about the curriculum. Make sure to find one that fits your child.

It's important not to hold back girls who love math. Often, girls are discouraged from using and loving math. It's a big problem in our society and in the U.S. in general. Remember that if they don't go on to college or start a career, they will still be better home educators for having learned math. If they do go on to college and career, they will be more likely to get college scholarships by having learned advanced math topics.

Chapter 3

# Social Studies

Social studies is another subject required for four years. In fact, social studies is the one area where colleges are fairly specific about what they want. They want to see American history (unless you live in a different country, in which case they want to see the history of your own country), world history, government or comparative governments, and economics. In some states, a state history class will be required, but not always.

Optional courses might include any of the social sciences, and there are many of them. Some of the social sciences include: psychology, sociology, anthropology, and comparative government. You could teach the history of anything or any country. Sometimes, it's helpful to look back at your high school classes, and think about what you took. One of the light-weight classes I took in my public high school was a class called "Polynesian History." Again, your options are limited only by your child's passions, but in public high school it's limited by the teacher's passions. My high school teacher was passionate about going to Hawaii every year, and he could help finance that trip to Hawaii by teaching a class called "Polynesian History." The options are endless!

This doesn't mean you shouldn't also cover the four required classes. If your child wants to branch out and try something different, that is completely fine. You can also use delight directed learning. If you find your child has a particular interest, you might want to look at The Teaching Company website (www.thegreatcourses.com). They offer college level lectures in audio and video formats, so your child can listen to the audio courses while you're driving around to different activities, or they can watch the videos.

There are some hands-on ways to get social sciences. For American government, look into Teen Pact or YMCA Youth and Government. It's a fun way to get information without a textbook. They can also work as a page at your state or local capital, or they might get involved in governments or elections. In our area, my sons participated in the Youth in Government program. It helped them learn about state government, but also gave them useful leadership experience - another important characteristic colleges look for.

Regardless of what you choose, the social sciences are a playground for the academically inclined and the intellectually curious. Enjoy exploring!

Chapter 4

# Science

Most colleges want to see three or four years of science, with one a lab science. Each area of science is so different, that a child may hate one but love the other, so it's helpful to try to expose them to different branches of science. Common science courses include biology, chemistry, and physics, but you can also include general or physical science. You don't necessarily have to cover general science; you can dive right into biology when your child is in ninth grade, if they're ready.

There are a million optional courses, limited only by your child's interests. You can teach the science of anything, or consider the general sciences; astronomy, geology, botany, and ecology are options I see fairly often. You can also cover science through delight directed learning. I know one homeschool boy who loved mycology, which is the study of mushrooms. This boy is now getting his PhD. Another child I know studied ornithology (the study of birds) every year. You can also branch out and study microbiology or animal husbandry. Many kids who own real working animals or who are involved in 4-H, study animal husbandry year after year. Others study horticulture or botany.

Before I became The HomeScholar (and before I homeschooled), I was a registered nurse. I loved being a nurse; I loved biology and chemistry. I'm a homeschool mom who loves science! Although I'm beginning to realize that not all homeschoolers feel the same way. In my work now, I get many questions about teaching homeschool high school science, particularly about science labs.

But what is a lab science? Can anyone tell me?

The truth is, there is no national definition about what a lab science is. No definition. The U.S. House of Representatives Committee on Science and Technology formed the Subcommittee on Research and Science Education that issued a report about lab science, and it is remarkably clear in its conclusion.

National Research Council's "America's Lab Report: Investigations in High School Science" states:

> "The NRC report committee concluded that there exists no commonly agreed upon definition of laboratories in high schools amongst researchers and educators."

How's that?!

Most colleges do not require documented lab sciences, although some colleges do. The most important thing is to research the schools where your child plans to apply. Usually a college that has specific science requirements also provides a method for them to be met. Perhaps they allow the ACT science portion to meet the requirement, or they accept an SAT Subject Test or AP exam in science.

## Science Requirements

In general, when I look over college preparation sites, they don't mention taking a lab science every year. Even the College Board doesn't specifically mention lab science. It mentions three years of science, but isn't specific about a lab requirement. Here is one example from a college:

> "Science teaches students to think analytically and apply theories to reality. Laboratory classes let students test what they have learned through hands-on work. Six semesters are recommended.
>
> - Two semesters in biology
> - Two semesters in chemistry and/or physics
> - Two semesters in earth/space sciences, advanced biology,

advanced      chemistry,      or physics"

Public universities may have a greater or lesser emphasis on lab science, depending on their preferences. But I think it's good to remember that colleges are rarely specific about *which* sciences, and it's OK for parents to include some delight-directed science courses along with the more ordinary biology-chemistry-physics choices.

## How to Find Curriculum

I always encourage parents to use what works for their students, because not all children learn the same way. It's more important that a curriculum *works* than that it is popular, inexpensive, or highly rated. When you are looking for a high school science course, look at Home Science Tools (hometrainingtools.com).

Make sure to get feedback from your student. They may be interested in a science that is slightly off the beaten track. Perhaps your child would prefer astronomy, geology, ecology, robotics, or equine science. Choose a textbook provider, such as Bob Jones or A Beka. You can change to an experiment-based model, such as TOPS or Rainbow Science. Consider pairing up with another homeschool family and completing science together. Your children don't have to be exactly the same age, and this can be especially helpful for children who enjoy socializing.

## Teaching Lab Science

Let me tell you a little about how I taught my children lab science. Remember, I used to work as a nurse, and I love biology. I loved every dissection and every microscopy lab. Sometimes I had trouble giving up the microscope for my children to use, but I don't believe I taught them anything. I *was* present in the room when they did their experiments. Biology labs include expensive microscope equipment and wielding sharp dissection tools, after all. Not wanting them to get hurt, I was always in the room. They read the labs on their own, they followed the directions, and I watched – usually while getting some laundry folded.

Once complete, I left them alone to complete the lab write-ups. I asked them for a paragraph on what they did and learned, and a drawing, graph, or chart explaining the lab. At the end of the day, I would look at their lab report to make sure they truly wrote a paragraph (not a sentence) and included some sort of chart or drawing. If everything was present and I understood from their lab report the purpose of the experiment and the result, then I gave them 100%.

To tell you the truth, I gave them a grade for the lab report based on how pleased or annoyed I felt when I saw it! After taking biology, chemistry, and physics at home, using this lab write-up philosophy, my children were *well* prepared for college science labs.

The science lab notebooks we used were cheap, spiral bound notebooks from the Target back-to-school sales. You could also use printer paper or regular notebook paper, because the lab notebook isn't about the *notebook* at all! The science lab notebook is about your child recording what they did during science lab.

When it was time for a test, I simply handed my children the test, confiscated the solution manual, and walked away. I corrected the tests when they were working on their next course. I gave them each a grade, and wrote it on a piece of notebook paper I kept in their binders. Then I had them correct their answers.

I suppose you could say they were learning independently. They did all the reading, and I didn't lecture (except about how expensive the microscope was). They did the experiments with an adult standing by. Perhaps I did try to teach them how fun and exciting biology is, because I remember I did a lot of squealing, but it didn't work. Of all the sciences, they liked biology the least.

I know other successful mothers who take a much more hands-on approach. Dealing with learning challenges, they may read the entire chapter, or carefully assist their child in following directions for labs. It's important to remember to do what works for *your* family. Some parents may want to judge others, and call it "spoon-feeding." I think it's important to remember that some students learn and thrive through one-on-one tutoring, because of challenges others don't understand, so do what works for your student, regardless of what others say or think.

## Many Options

There are many options for lab sciences. You are not limited to the common three choices of biology, chemistry, and physics. While the core sciences are probably helpful for students going into highly competitive schools, or going into science and engineering schools, you don't have to be limited by those standard three. Some students will not have the math required for physics, and others may want to branch out. They both have limitless options!

When faced with a non-math child, skipping physics and physics lab may be a good idea, because it's highly math-based. If you decide to branch out into nature study, a field study can be your lab. Even though there is no definition of "lab science," the term does imply hands-on learning and writing a description of what was accomplished. There are public schools that teach botany and ecology classes that may fit the bill. Earth sciences may also be a lab science, provided you do some experiments. The good news is you can make almost *any* science into a hands-on experience.

Chapter 5

# Economics

I have a son who loves economics, and who earned a BA in the subject. Personally, I failed two classes in college: calculus and economics. As a result, whenever I have a question on economics, I often turn to my son to straighten me out. When we studied it in high school (okay, when *he* studied it), I was surprised to learn that economics comes with a worldview attached. Often, we think about worldview in terms of philosophy, religion (or possibly biology, if you're interested in the creation/evolution debate). Most of the time, we don't include economics in this list, but it does have a worldview, so keep it in mind when you consider a curriculum. Books usually represent the author's worldview and political persuasion, and it can be difficult to find a perspective that matches your own.

Economics falls under the category of the social sciences, and there are multiple kinds, such as micro, macro, marketing, and business economics. Even if your child doesn't plan to work or study in the field of economics as an adult, it's important to have a basic understanding of it, because economic theories and ideas play a role in so many different areas of life. Working at a business? They need to understand economics. Voting for tax increases or discussing the federal debt? They need to understand economics. Planning to file income tax returns?! They need to understand economics.

If your student loves reading, there is one curriculum that my son recommends called Economics in a Box. For visual learners, The Teaching Company offers a course called "Basic Economics." We used this curriculum with our older son, who doesn't like economics. I got to junior year in high school, and suddenly realized that although my younger son had three years of economics, my older one had zero credits in economics, so I needed a fast fix. We got The Teaching Company's "Basic Economics" course, and I had him listen to it. It was a quick and easy way for him to learn economics. Another resource we used was the book, *Economics in One Lesson* by Henry Hazlitt. If you have a little more time to spend on economics, or have a student who enjoys it, be sure to look at Founders Academy online classes which promise U.S. History and Economics in half the time without the tears (www.foundersacademy.net).

If you truly hate economics, you can't stand to make a big purchase, or your child does better with workbooks, then another option is the book, *Whatever Happened to Penny Candy?* which can be used along with a separate workbook. I've heard from numerous sources that it is a good half credit economics course, especially for early high school students.

Chapter 6

# Foreign Languages

The college prep requirement for foreign language is two to three years for a single language. It's not going to help a lot if you do one year of Spanish, one year of French, and one year of Latin, as colleges want to see one consistent language. In order to be successful in one foreign language, make sure your student studies for a bare minimum of 15 minutes every single day all year round during school days, five days a week.

There are many language courses to choose from. Colleges almost always accept Latin. It's excellent for math-minded children. Colleges often (but not always) accept American Sign Language. They usually do not accept other sign languages; ASL is the one they will accept.

I've noticed an interesting difference between the U.S. and other countries. An exchange student once told me that in Germany, the public schools teach several foreign languages by the time students graduate. They teach English starting from kindergarten or first grade, then French. In high school, students learn another language, and usually become conversant in several languages by graduation. You might say that would count as cheating, since they live in Europe, and can drive around different countries to speak with native speakers ... but it does point out a difference between the U.S. and other countries. This is one of the reasons why U.S. citizens are sometimes called "arrogant Americans," because they don't learn the languages of other countries they visit. Foreign languages can help you if your child wants to travel, whether for military, missionary, or vacation purposes. By learning the language, they won't be labeled an "arrogant American."

If you are a family living overseas and your children have become bilingual, or if you're a bilingual family, you can give your child high school credit for languages they learn naturally. Just because you don't beat them over the head with a textbook (!) doesn't mean they don't deserve credit for what they learn. If your child learned to play the piano naturally, you'd give them piano credit. I suggest you give credit for foreign language learned, as well. Document some of the foreign language they learn naturally by demonstrating they've used that foreign language in community service, or have passed a test in foreign language such as CLEP or AP Spanish.

If your child is an interpreter for American Sign Language at your church, this may be proof they are relatively bilingual. Or if your child is interpreting Armenian in your Armenian church, it can demonstrate your child is bilingual.

If you are missing a foreign language, which sometimes does happen, there are some things you can do. Some colleges don't require foreign languages. Some require a foreign language only for specific majors. There are some colleges that will waive the requirement for foreign language. It's worth looking into. Some colleges require foreign language for the purpose of graduating college, but not necessarily to get in. They may waive the requirement to get into college, but require that your child take two years of foreign language in college.

There's also a quick fix for foreign language. You can do an intensive study, seven days a week, using Rosetta Stone for an hour or more a day. It doesn't matter how quickly you get to the second level, it's the second level that matters. There's always the option of community college, but community college is an R-rated environment, and you should be especially careful with foreign languages. At our local community college, professors help students experience French culture by showing R-rated French movies containing nudity.

Chapter 7

# Physical Education

Usually, colleges require two years of physical education. It's fine if your child earns half a credit each year. Your child can earn P.E. credits naturally. Your child can learn about health, go camping or hiking, participate in Boy Scouts, learn first aid or CPR, enjoy cycling, or participate in individual or team sports. You can even include dance. Frankly, that can be helpful for kids who don't enjoy typical sports. They may turn up their noses at sports activities, camping, or hiking, but they can dance all day long.

When thinking about P.E., use this rule of thumb: anything that breaks a sweat counts as P.E. Whether your child is skateboarding or involved in a team sport, it doesn't matter; anything that breaks a sweat counts!

If you have a student who wants to get into a military academy, documentation of physical fitness may be needed. This doesn't mean you have to sign your child up for football at the public high school; any measured fitness activity counts. This could include team sports, but it can also be measured by a time achieved in a race, such as a marathon. Your student's fitness could be measured by their involvement in an individual sport, such as a black belt in martial arts, or they could win an award in a competition.

If your child is interested in a military academy, sometimes they have particular needs for different sports. If your child hasn't chosen something they love doing, or are ready to try a new sport, ask the military academy what type of sport they would like to see. Once, when I was at a college fair, an academy asked me for a particular sport; they had a specific sport in mind, and were willing to give a good scholarship for it.

## The Education in P.E.

If you have a student who would rather sit than break a sweat, you can focus on the "education" side of Physical Education. In other words, teach them "Health." One curriculum I recommend is *Total Health*. This is a complete high school curriculum that covers many things that promote health.

- *Total Health: Talking About Life's Changes* is a health textbook for middle school students.
- *Total Health, Choices for a Winning Lifestyle* is a health textbook for high school students.

Part of your health course may include instruction on dating and relationships. These books are from a Christian perspective:

- *I Kissed Dating Goodbye* by Joshua Harris

- *Boy Meets Girl: Say Hello to Courtship* by Joshua Harris
- *Boundaries in Dating* by Henry Cloud and John Townsend

Chapter 8

# Fine Arts

Your student's high school records should include one credit of fine arts. Not being an artistic family, we had to look up "fine arts" in the dictionary. What I learned is that fine arts are music, art, theater, and dance. Who knew?

There is a wide array of opportunities to find these credits. Some choose music or art lessons, but there are more budget-conscious ways to get the credits. My kids didn't like hands on projects, so we studied fine arts through history using library books. We studied music history by checking out CDs and biographical books on different composers and styles of music.

You can combine your activities, such as music, art, theater, or dance, and call it a one-year course. Or you can teach one year of piano to cover fine arts. If you combine activities, you could call it "Survey of Fine Arts" or "Introduction to Fine Arts." There usually isn't a pre-measured book or curriculum that you can use to count credit hours, so keep in mind that an hour a day, or 120-180 hours of work, is equal to one credit.

You will learn quickly that if your child is interested in fine arts, you may find yourself with the "too many credits" problem. But in a public school setting, it is also possible for a child who likes the fine arts to have "too many credits." I had plenty of friends in high school who took both choir and band. In some schools, they may be in choir, band and orchestra! If your child has more than one credit of fine arts, that's fine, if it's what your child truly loves doing.

When I took choir in high school, it fulfilled my fine arts requirement, and it was on my high school transcript as music. I also had choir on my transcript activity list. If you use an activity as a class, it doesn't mean you can't also put it on the activity list as an activity. You can't use the same class for two different credits, but your child can receive credit and have it listed as an activity.

Chapter 9

# Electives

High school graduation requirements may include 18 to 20 high school credits. College preparation requirements may include 22 to 24 credits. Once you fill up the core classes, where do you get the other credits? From electives! Delight directed learning can give enough electives to demonstrate your child's passions. You can also assign electives. Some classes may not be core classes, but they are still required.

## Family Requirements

High school requirements vary between homeschoolers. You may put state required classes in the electives category, or include classes that are required by your family. Some families require Bible or religion classes. Some parents require their child to have a personal finance, driver education, or consumer math credit. Others require home economics, auto mechanics, or entrepreneur skills. Each family is unique.

Some colleges may like to see religion or Bible classes. Some religious schools like to know that your child has background in the Old and New Testament. Other colleges won't accept your religion classes. Put on the transcript what you know to be honest and true; if a school chooses to take these classes out of the GPA calculation or deduct them from your child's total number of credits, that's fine.

Some family requirements involve an educational philosophy. An interest in logic, rhetoric, and critical thinking may lead to classes that are mandatory for your family. If they don't fit in another category, these classes may be categorized as electives.

# Counting Hours

When you don't use a pre-measured curriculum, determine credit value for your elective classes by counting hours. As long as your hours fall within 120 to 180 hours of work, you can count it as a whole high school credit.

You don't necessarily have to use a textbook; you can create classes on your own. Your job is to put on the transcript what you know to be honest and true. This is particularly true for electives. Include what your student has done during high school.

# State Requirements

State laws vary, so check your state laws to see whether there are any required homeschool classes. Some classes may not be core requirements, and can be considered elective. In my state, for example, occupational education is required. Other states may have a computer science or technology requirement.

If your state law requires an elective, you can use the name of the requirement for the title of your class. If "Occupational Education" is required, then use the class title, "Occupational Education." Another state may require online learning, and that can be the name of your class.

Meeting a requirement for occupational education is easy. At a certain point, your teenager will become motivated by money, whether it's to pay for their cell phone or for spending money. When they find a job, count the hours on the job, name your class based on the law or by using the title of their job.

## Natural Learning

A certain amount of natural learning can be included on your transcript as an elective credit. Your child may be on the computer all the time. If they're doing a lot of photo editing online, or blogging, or gaming, this can often indicate computer skills they have. You can build on their knowledge with some intentional learning to add to their high school credits. Say, "I want you to sit down and learn how to type using the home keys." They might learn how to use Microsoft Office (Word, PowerPoint, and Excel).

If your child is learning naturally, try to come up with a class title by talking with them. If they are working on the computer a lot, for example, ask your children what they're doing and listen for strange words you don't understand. These strange words may become a class title. A simple clarifying question such as, "Wait, what is it that you just said?" can make all the difference. They may go on to list a computer language they are using or software they have figured out. Have them spell it out for you and then look it up to try to figure out what it is. That can become part of your class title, such as "Computer Science - HTML Basics" or "Computer Science - C++ Basics."

Chapter 10

# 10 No-fail Strategies for Choosing Curriculum

If you're feeling a bit insecure when you start high school, how do you go about choosing curriculum? Here are ten proven strategies to help you make successful curriculum decisions. If you're still stuck, I'll share my personal starting points for choosing curriculum, so you can see what I used.

## Strategy 1: Use What Works

Look back at your successful homeschool years and think about the curriculum you used that worked. Find a curriculum that is similar. Your mantra should be, "If it works, keep using it." The grass will always be greener on the other side of the fence, but maybe that grass is Astroturf! If your grass is already green, don't look somewhere else.

When I work with clients, I always suggest they keep using a curriculum that works. If Sonlight has always worked for you, keep using Sonlight. Of course, the flip side is also true. If something is *not* working, start looking around for something else. Even if you are in the middle of a school year, once you recognize a curriculum isn't working, change as *soon* as possible. It will save you so much frustration!

## Strategy 2: Do What Works

When you are looking for something new, how do you know where to begin? As you shop for curriculum, your family's learning styles can help guide your choices. If your child works best with workbooks, then keep using what works (see Strategy 1). In high school, some students will do their schoolwork in notebooks. If your child has done well with hands-on projects, keep using them!

Even in the high school years, there are plenty of natural learning opportunities: Boy Scouts, 4-H, *Patty Paper Geometry*, and YMCA Youth and Government are all great hands-on learning. Look around until you find a match for your child's learning style. My children learned best through reading. Whenever I got stuck with a curriculum that didn't work, we went back to our roots - reading. Sometimes the curriculum choice flat out didn't work - art comes to mind! That's when we read about the topic instead, which meant reading books about art history.

"Do what works" can also mean using a curriculum provider you have used in the past. I used Sonlight Curriculum, and it was perfect for our family. When I decided to try teaching Latin, I used the program that Sonlight provides. I figured that if Sonlight was working for me, then I could trust their people to choose a good Latin program. So, if it worked for and looked good to them, it would probably work for me as well. Place a higher value on recommendations from curriculum suppliers that work for you.

## Strategy 3: Use Homeschool Curriculum

A textbook written for a public or private school assumes the teacher already understands the subject. A book written for homeschoolers assumes the teacher knows *nothing* about the subject! This is why homeschool curriculum is easier to use and makes you feel competent instead of stupid. Curriculum written for homeschoolers doesn't assume your child is in a classroom setting or suggest impractical group projects. When you use a curriculum meant for homeschooling, you can teach the subject without help, even when you don't have a clue about the content. My children learned physics and calculus without any help from me! We were successful because we used the formula "homeschool curriculum + their effort = success."

# Strategy 4: Get Self-Teaching Curriculum

Homeschool curriculum works because it's usually self-teaching. Your ultimate goal is *not* to be the "teacher" of a subject. Your long-term plan is to raise a learner who can absorb material by themselves. A self-teaching curriculum will prepare your student for college and life. It will help you teach what you don't know, and help your child learn subjects primarily on their own. When your student goes to college, they will need to absorb college textbooks by themselves. Choosing a self-teaching curriculum will give them the practice they need in order to do so.

## Strategy 5: Don't Start Over

Most curriculum suppliers think their curriculum is the living end. They think it is the best, teaches the best, that their way is the right way, and that without them you can't possibly learn all you need to know. A writing program may tell you to start at level one, even though your student is in high school, so the student will follow their program completely. A math program may tell you that even a ninth grader should start their curriculum by learning basic addition. There are probably some good reasons for starting over, and you will know if this is important for your child.

On the other hand, starting over is *not* always important or advisable. For example, when a curriculum offers a placement test, there is no reason to start at the beginning. I have seen parents start over with a different math program every year, putting their child further and further behind. Resist the urge to start over when you purchase a new curriculum. Start where it makes sense for *your* child.

## Strategy 6: Focus on Specialization

Buy a curriculum that covers all the basics. You can't skimp on reading, writing, math, science, and social studies. On the other hand, you also want to choose a curriculum that will encourage their passion! If your child loves art, music, or science, remember to buy a curriculum for those subjects!

I'm reminded of the Bible verse, "If his son shall ask for bread, will he give him a stone?" (Matthew 7:9.) If your child *asks* for a subject, give it to them! If they ask for microbiology, or economics, or Russian history, follow their interests and get it for them. Try to avoid taking a passion and making it a "school subject" though. I remember a client who wanted to encourage her student's interest, so she turned it into a homeschool course - complete with assignments, worksheets, and tests. Strangely enough, her student lost interest in the subject when it became a dreaded class he had to work on. Don't make your child's specialization a subject, simply let them enjoy it. Then when they are done, put it on the transcript!

## Strategy 7: Invest In Your Weaknesses

Where is the best place to put your hard-earned curriculum money? Invest in your weaknesses! If you hate math, you don't know what you're doing in the subject, and you avoid it at all costs, then *that* is where to put your money. Strengths are fun to finance, and areas of specialization will often result in birthday and Christmas presents. But purchasing things for your weaknesses take conscious effort. What do you hate teaching? In which subjects do you feel like you're failing? Those are the best places to put your curriculum dollars. If you need to, you could teach all the "fun stuff" in the library and using real life, but weak areas may need a little extra help.

## Strategy 8: Allow Teens to Choose

It can be helpful to let your teen choose curriculum - *especially* in their weak areas. As your teen progresses, try to engage them in choosing curriculum. If you can come up with two or three suitable alternatives for a subject and you can't decide, then perhaps your teen can place the deciding vote. This will often help to reduce whining about curriculum. After all, who can they blame? They chose it themselves!

This strategy is especially important when you are looking at a video curriculum of any kind. Teens are remarkably sensitive to visual programs. Things that look fine to us may drive them crazy! Maybe it's the way a speaker dresses or the sound of their voice, but sometimes a video annoys kids so much they can't learn. Whenever possible, have your teen compare video samples and make their own choice. Even without a video, you may still be surprised by their choices. I remember being stunned when my son chose Saxon math! Believe it or not, he was looking for a book with pages full of math problems. Meanwhile, I had been shopping for a curriculum with clearly written instructions and colorful photos and diagrams. Let your teen help you choose curriculum, and you could be pleasantly surprised.

## Strategy 9: Invest in Yourself

Each year, spend some of your curriculum dollars on yourself. Invest your money in keeping yourself organized, knowledgeable, and excited about teaching. When my oldest was in seventh grade, I started buying myself a book about high school each year. By the time he started ninth grade, I understood the basics of high school. I kept investing in myself each year. I learned about college admission, scholarships, and high school tests. I learned about being the guidance counselor, and homeschooling college courses. If books aren't your thing, invest in some consulting. I know of a good homeschool consultant, so if you need one, check out my Gold Care Club!

I found that everything I spent on myself ended up saving our family a lot in the long run. Because of my studies, my kids won scholarships through our English program, and their college essays brought wonderful financial aid. Investing in yourself will help you feel more confident now, but can also reap wonderful long-term rewards.

## Strategy 10: Tried and True

As you look at curriculum choices, try to choose something tried and true. Do you remember the crisis over "New Math" in public schools? Have you ever wondered why public school budgets are so high while schools are throwing away perfectly good curriculum? Schools are always on the lookout for the latest and greatest, and lose sight of the tried and true curriculum. Frankly, this is a rut homeschoolers can fall into as well. You want the new edition, the updated version, and the latest curriculum. But at what cost? The book *may* be a good new curriculum, it's true. It might also stink.

If you have some extra money and the latest and greatest is important to you, then feel free to get the newest choices. If you have the money to correct any duds, there is no harm in that! If you don't have the financial flexibility to make frequent mistakes, then consider using only tried and true curriculum.

# Conclusion: Starting Points

If you have no idea where to start, then look for clues around you. Look at your homeschooling friends. What do they use? Does it look good? Do you trust their judgment? Do their kids seem to be learning? Look at curriculum suppliers you know and trust. If you trust them for science, perhaps you could try their history program. Research similar curriculum choices on the Internet. If your child likes video tutorials for math, try finding a video tutorial for foreign language. Look for award winners. You can find award winners in magazines such as "The Old Schoolhouse" and books such as *102 Top Picks for Homeschool Curriculum* by Cathy Duffy (of Cathy Duffy Reviews) or through homedexpert.com.

If you don't even know where to begin, or if you haven't homeschooled before, then you can try my curriculum favorites and see if they fit your family. I used Sonlight Curriculum, because it is geared to learning through reading. Although we used it in the traditional way, their boxes of books could provide a year of unschooling for a student who loves to read.

I used ROCK Solid when I searched for new subjects, because they don't offer an overwhelming number of choices on their website - only a few of each. Home Science Tools was my favorite provider for lab science, because they have science ideas for every subject in every age group *and* great customer service.

You are your child's love-giver. You are the one who knows them best. Nobody else can tell you what curriculum to use without their biases shading their opinions. Use what you know about your child to make your decisions. Invest in their future by putting your money into yourself and your weaknesses first. Provide the basics, of course, but also invest in your child's loves and interests. You know your child, and you can make better decisions with your money than anyone else!

Chapter 11

# A Grouch-free Guide to Grading English

Parents are often nervous about high school subjects, and English is one of the more intimidating courses - at least it was for me. Editing and grading papers can be a *huge* hassle! As I describe how I graded in our homeschool, I hope these ideas will be an encouragement and inspiration to you.

Let me describe our "Journal Writing" course first. Sounds impressive, right? I bought a blank book and told my sons to fill one page of the blank book each day. They only had to show it to me from across the room, so I could see they had written something and filled the page. I didn't read over what they wrote. This allowed them to keep their journals relatively private, while I could still be sure they were writing in their own handwriting each day. That was easy, right? But what about "real" papers?

During our early high school years, I was in charge of editing the papers. Day after day, I required our sons to write. They spent an hour a day writing (the goal being to produce a one to two page paper each week). They were good about writing. I was good about making sure they turned it in. Dad was good about playing the heavy and ensuring the paper was turned in on Friday each week. That's about where it all fell apart. I never seemed to edit the papers. I would read them and get frustrated, and not know where to even *begin* editing the papers. I put it on my calendar, but still didn't get around to editing them often.

Finally, seeing me flounder, my husband rode in and saved the day! What a huge relief! I felt enormously guilty, because I am good at English. My husband is an engineer - I should have been getting help from him in science and math, right? But the editing was something he was interested in helping with, and it lightened my load considerably. We shared the same philosophy on editing - which is, of course, that kids should learn to write.

What does editing look like? In our house, my husband read the papers once through, from beginning to end. Then he went back and started over, correcting spelling, grammar, and punctuation. He made comments such as, "This isn't quite clear" or "What are you trying to say?" or "Run on sentence" or "Use more descriptive terms." Then he returned the papers, and our children were required to correct all the edits. Once corrected, they earned their grades for the papers. If they corrected the edits well, the grade was an "A." If they corrected the edits, but didn't do well, then they got a "B". Each child was graded based on their own writing ability, using our family mantra, "Never compare - someone always gets hurt."

Our philosophy on learning to write is that practice makes perfect. Practice, practice, practice! Have your child write every day - greeting cards, blog posts, and journal entries! It's more important than what curriculum you choose. We also believe that editing is part of the writing process. My husband worked at a large company and as they prepared proposals, entire teams of engineers wrote, rewrote, and edited each other's work. It's part of life. So he edited their papers like he edited papers at work.

We practiced with a paper each week, along with journal writing. Toward the end of high school, we also taught them how to complete hand-written essays in 25 minutes, so they would succeed in the SAT test (although these days the essay test in the SAT is longer). We didn't edit these essays; my husband commented on them and graded them. We used the book *501 Writing Prompts* by Learning Express, which has a nice explanation of how to grade a short essay.

Each writer has their own "voice." When my son entered the honors program at his university, the professor commented on my son's writing voice. He said that my son was obviously used to reading quality literature. Whew! All that literature-based education worked! My son got his writing voice through reading! Yes, voice is important. When you edit, try to keep your corrections to two things: mechanics and clarity. Mechanics means punctuation, grammar, spelling, and other conventions. Clarity means you can understand what they mean. Much of the rest of writing can be the writer's voice. You can talk to them about their voice, and ask them to write for different purposes and in different styles (first person, narrative, etc.), but they can still have a voice of their own.

We used Sonlight curriculum for writing. Even when we stopped using Sonlight (because we had already read all of the books!), we continued to use their writing plan. It helped to know how much writing to schedule each week. It helped me provide a variety of different assignments each year. So we used and re-used their writing plan, and I varied the subject of each assignment.

Often, I let my children decide what to write about. For example, they could write about *any* novel they had read during the year, or write about *any* subject area they were studying in school, not only history. Again, my goal was for them to learn to write, and I felt they would learn more if they enjoyed it. Letting them choose the subject of each assignment was a way for them to enjoy writing more. (No, they didn't like hard work any more than the next kid, but they did seem to tolerate it better when they could choose the subject.)

They sometimes wrote too much on a subject they loved. Toward the end of the year, my instructions were more specific: "You can write on anything, but nothing involving anyone on Mt. Rushmore." By letting them choose their subject, and guiding them to choose a variety of subjects, we ended up with a written paper in almost every course each year. It was helpful when I needed something to document subjects such as art, music, and economics.

Writing instruction varies widely between families. If a curriculum or instruction method is working well for you and your children, then keep using it. If you have struggled to find the right one, then keep looking, but also remember that *practice* writing is most important. Getting feedback on written work will ultimately improve writing the most.

Appendix 1

# How to Cope with a Lack of Motivation in Teens

It can happen overnight. One day your child is pleasant, cooperative, and enthusiastic about learning. The next day ... not so much. It happens to boys and girls, but not to everyone. It's common, but that doesn't make it easier for parents to deal with. What do you do with a child who will only do the bare minimum, and isn't interested in learning?

Some teenagers remain pleasant and generally cooperative, but do everything in a uniquely slow-as-molasses way, with a seemingly complete lack of motivation. This is when parents look heavenward, asking the age-old question, "Now what?"

Sometimes this may be "just a phase," - as if your child is checking to see who the boss *is*, and what *matters* to Mom and Dad. If that is the case, then the solution is to wait until the phase is over ... Bummer, I know, because as a parent, it feels like nails on the chalkboard all day, every day. Sometimes it lasts a couple of weeks, while the child (or parent) figures out what adjustments have to be made. Other times, the lack of motivation lasts for months - or even a year - until the child finds something that sparks an interest.

## Misery Loves Company

One of my clients, Cindy, was devastated when her daughter became this way at age 14. Her daughter had always been a driven perfectionist. But suddenly her daughter wasn't interested in piano or flute any longer, and didn't enjoy any activity. Cindy was worried about her uncharacteristically sitting around on the couch all day. Finally, her daughter picked up a guitar for the first time ... and a few months later, she was helping the worship leader at church. When I spoke to Cindy recently, she hardly remembered those difficult times.

Another client had a similar concern. I was consulting with her in her home, and I met her son. He had no interests but the couch and video games - she was beside herself. I saw this client a few months ago, and her son had completely turned the corner. She "forced" him to take a class for school, and he suddenly discovered politics and debate. Now he is going 100% full speed.

I know that I had issues, particularly with my oldest. At the time, his love of chess *seemed* to be wasting his life doing nothing. He sat on the couch reading books about chess, and playing that crazy board game for hours on end. At the time, I thought I would go nuts. Now, of course, I realize he was working on his area of specialization, but at the time it was horrible.

Other moms have gone through this same thing and survived. It doesn't make it easier, but perhaps it can make it more tolerable. Beyond knowing that misery loves company, I can offer some possible solutions. Take what will work for your family.

## Assess Your Expectations

Is your teen lacking motivation to learn? Assess the expectations you have in your homeschool. Sometimes, when I consult with moms about this issue and talk to them at length, I find out the child is overworked. If you are giving your child a classical education, particularly at a classical homeschool co-op, you may be at greater risk of having expectations that are too high. Regardless of your curriculum choice, look at the schoolwork you are expecting.

Is the level of work too high? Are the number of hours too great? How many hours would it take a normal child to work at normal speed to get that amount of work done? How long would it take you to complete all the assignments, if you were doing them at a normal speed? Is your child expected to work longer at school than your spouse spends at work?

The opposite may also be true, when the expectations are too low. When kids are bored, it's hard to get motivated to do anything. If your child is working with younger siblings, your child is gifted, or you are using a curriculum meant for younger grades, then you may be at greater risk. Homeschool co-ops and multi-age curriculum are wonderful things for homeschoolers much of the time, but parents still need to assess wonderful things. If something isn't working, you have to find out what is wrong before you can fix it.

## Raising Real Men

If you have a son, this stage may be a unique attempt to become a man. It's difficult to grow from "boy" to "man" when you don't have meaningful work and you aren't the alpha-male and top-dog of the home. My husband made a short YouTube video, "Raising Boys vs. Raising Men." This resource may help you think about possible causes and solutions.

My sons each obtained a meaningful job at about 14 years old. This is one of the benefits of homeschooling, because you do have more flexibility to incorporate employment into your school day. We did school four days a week, allowing the fifth day for them to spend working. Is there something your son has been saying he wants to do? Can you find a situation, or a mentor to help him do it?

Some parents have confessed that, while their child wanted to do something, they couldn't allow it because they didn't have time. The opposite may be true. If you do *not* do things that give meaning, they may work on school more slowly because they are bored and frustrated. Avoiding unique opportunities can add to the problem. Therefore, one possible solution might be searching for some meaningful, "real adult" kind of work. Some parents work from home, and will start to include their son in work activities. Others will allow work-related activities or mentors.

# The Specialization Solution

It may simply have to do with a lack of specialization. Young people need something they are good at. They want to be known as "the kid who..." Adults will say to each other, "Where do you work?" or "What do you do?" Children want their own "thing" so they can grow up. The problem is that young adults don't have much exposure to the world, and sometimes they haven't stumbled upon a special interest yet.

The solution to a lack of specialization is exposing children to a wide variety of experiences and subjects through a liberal arts education, and plenty of time to do new things. I must confess that it can take a long time before something "clicks." Many people suggest speech and debate or involvement in political organizations as your first attempt at something new. For young people, these activities give them an opportunity to speak their mind and argue - without arguing with their parents - and it can improve their sense of self.

Look carefully at a lack of specialization as a possible cause. When I see a parent with this problem, they often miss important clues about their child's interests. One way to identify specialization is to pay attention to what annoys you. You can use your "annoy-o-meter" to recognize specialization that may be hidden below the surface. I have written an article on this topic that may help.

## Use Your Annoy-O-Meter Skillfully

Give your child more input into their activities and involvements. Perhaps they should quit Boy Scouts – or not! Instead they may want to quit the sports club. Would your child prefer acting or computer programming instead of the activities you have provided?

## Cause and Effect Strategy

When I had toddlers, I spent a lot of time thinking about natural consequences. I wanted to provide real world, cause and effect reasons for my children to behave. Using this same strategy, try to brainstorm ideas that will have a direct cause and effect result in your teenager. The key is a simple if-then statement presented in a matter-of-fact way.

Effective suggestions:
- IF you text while driving THEN you are not mature enough to use my car.
- IF you are too tired to do school THEN you are too tired to have friends over.

Ineffective suggestion:
- IF you don't do your work THEN Mom will pitch a fit.

## High Quality Problems

Motivation problems can occur even in wonderful children with great attitudes. My son Kevin was like that - always pleasant and cooperative. I remember when Kevin was a "terrible two" and didn't want to be in the shopping mall. He simply sat down and said, "No thank you, Mommy." He was so obedient and sweet! He was the same way at 14 years old. Saying, "No thank you, Mommy" to a math lesson doesn't work as well, though. At that age, they are too big for you to pick them up and remove them to an obedient situation.

The problems you face (along with many others) may be better problems, or on a completely different plane, than the problems many other parents face. Knowing that your problems are "good problems" rather than "bad problems" only helps a little. At its core, it is still a problem that causes stress and anxiety. Knowing you have a "good problem" isn't a solution, but perhaps it's an encouragement.

## Serious Trouble

I've been around the block a few times, though, and I know not everything is perfect in homeschool families. Sometimes problems are *huge* and *horrible*. Teenagers can make their own decisions. Sometimes they make the biggest, most horrendous decisions. Worse still, sometimes the consequences of their actions are life-altering. You may find encouragement from the Parenting Today's Teens with Mark Gregston website. He offers some free ebooks you can download, as well as regular podcasts and articles.

If you have a teen making ridiculously bizarre or unsafe decisions, place the blame squarely where it resides - with the teen. God designed people with free will. Sometimes children will act on their free will earlier than others. Try to evaluate for common problems. At the same time, be watchful for serious problems, such as depression, drug or alcohol use, pornography, gambling, bullying, or gaming. I've read that Internet addiction causes brain changes similar to alcohol and drugs.

One article gives strong warnings:

> "I have seen people who stopped attending university lectures, failed their degrees or their marriages broke down because they were unable to emotionally connect with anything outside the game. When

someone comes to you and says they did not sleep last night because they spent 14 hours playing games, and it was the same the previous night, and they tried to stop but they couldn't, you know they have a problem." (FoxNews.com/Health)

You can find more information on internet addiction in my book, *TechnoLogic: How to Set Logical Technology Boundaries and Stop the Zombie Apocalypse.*

Read my article, "What If? Homeschool High School Without Fear" for encouragement. Although the article was written for families facing trauma, it may bring encouragement and hope for families suffering through the trauma of truly horrendous teenage consequences.

## Bottom Line ...

Right now, your teen may seem to be making a horrendous waste of God-given potential, destined to live the loveless life of a vagabond. In truth though, they aren't.

- It's a phase.
- It will pass.
- It's not terminal.

# Appendix 2

# **Love with Strings Attached**

As a homeschooler, you have probably been getting quite a few emails from people who want you to stop homeschooling independently. These emails make many promises and are from parent partnership and alternative education programs. Whether they receive money from the government, or money directly from homeschoolers, these programs benefit financially when they make you feel inadequate and incapable. They love you – but there are strings attached. Don't let them make you feel less than qualified!

# Government Funding

When you accept public money, you give up some control in exchange. If you use a parent partnership homeschool program through a public school, the school may exert control over your child's education. These programs may claim to love homeschoolers for who they are, and may say they will not exert control over your homeschool, but they *can*. Alternative education programs could change their policies at any time. I have seen this happen – families will start with a program and feel happy with it – and then, the following year, the rules change.

These programs often require that you be evaluated by a teacher, spend a certain number of hours in a classroom, or submit work to be graded. They may require you to choose a curriculum from a certain list, or may not approve of your choice of curriculum. Many will not allow you to teach using your worldview, using a religious curriculum, or including religious instruction in your school day.

## The Real Teacher

Look at these advertisements and what they imply. Some ads say they offer "real teachers" – which of course implies that you aren't a real teacher. But you are a home educator, and that's as real as teaching can get. They also may state they use "approved curriculum" when your homeschool curriculum is approved, too – approved by the homeschool parent who knows their child best. I have also seen parent partnerships advertise a "real high school diploma," yet a homeschool diploma is real as well. In fact, my children's high school diplomas were real enough to earn college admission and scholarships. These programs may offer "accredited transcripts" when some public schools aren't accredited any more than homeschools are, and most colleges understand that your transcript is valid without accreditation.

## School at Home

These advertisements can look impressive, but I encourage you to look at the details. Programs like these provide a "school at home" experience that is not a good fit for many families. Families often homeschool to avoid the trappings of school. Here are a few advertising phrases I found interesting:

*"Curriculum is individualized."* However, the program only used the textbook, workbook, school-at-home style learning. Not every homeschooler chooses this method.

*"Outstanding curriculum with the expertise of your advisor."* The best guidance counselor is the parent, who knows and loves their child. And those "outstanding curriculum choices" may only include the limited options above.

*"Vocational to advanced placement."* You can provide this at home as well. Your homeschool can provide anything from AP courses to remedial education, as needed. Your homeschool is not

limited by curriculum choices, and can put together any class your student needs, at any level, no matter how strange or unusual your child's interests.

*"Record-keeping options."* You can include any educational experiences on your official homeschool transcript. Include a public school calculus or band class, a co-op class, a distance-learning class, and a community college class all on one official homeschool transcript. If you need help with this, check out my Total Transcript Solution at www.TotalTranscriptSolution.com. It is often less difficult to keep records when you homeschool independently, because you can do it your own way.

*"Tuition is only ..."* Perhaps it only costs $195 for the first student, but what if the fine print reveals additional costs of $1000 or more? It can be expensive.

## Learning Pace

Regardless of public or private school affiliations, parent partnership programs often have requirements on the rate of instruction. It may be too fast or two slow for your child. Since kids usually learn in fits and spurts, requiring a constant rate of learning can be either frustrating because it's too fast, or boring because it's too slow.

When I consider the steady rate of classroom teaching, I always think about that TV episode with Lucille Ball in the candy factory. She tries so hard to keep up, to the point of shoving candy into her hat, mouth, and blouse to show she isn't falling behind! When she works quickly, the conveyor belt moves faster, and she is never able to keep up. Homeschooling does not have to be that way. You can work at a comfortable pace, making sure it's challenging but not overwhelming.

## Fearless Homeschooling

Make sure any choices you make are based on what's right for your own child (because you know your child best), and *not* based on a fear of homeschooling. Fear is not a good reason for making choices about schooling options.

Sometimes parent partnership programs talk about how difficult the teenage years can be. Teenagers can be difficult, as all age groups can be difficult, as parenting in general is difficult. I'm not convinced these programs can do a better job of educating teens. I think some teens will be difficult no matter which method you choose.

Homeschool parents may not even consider parent partnership programs when their kids are younger. Sometimes, as they approach the high school years, their anxiety increases and they begin to listen to the voices suggesting they can't do it by themselves or insisting that the state can help them. The truth is you *can* homeschool high school without getting the government involved.

Beware of organizations that try to sell you something by playing on your fears or making you feel incompetent. This strategy is a dead giveaway that their motives are not pure, and they don't have your best interests at heart. Instead, listen to those who have homeschooled successfully before you, those who can encourage and support you and help you make your homeschool as good as it can be.

Accredited distance learning programs can be the right choice for some families, but look closely at the messages, weigh the pros and cons, and think carefully before choosing. Remember that you have no need to be afraid of homeschooling!

You *can* homeschool independently through high school! Thousands have before you and the rewards are incredible. There is help along the way! Your family will be blessed by your decision.

## Questions to Ask

Before you decide to give alternative education or parent partnership programs a try, ask yourself some questions:

- What am I going to have to give to receive what they promise?

- Do I feel inadequate when I read the ad or talk to the person?
- Do they stand to gain financially by making me feel inadequate?
- Will they be able to exert influence over what I teach my children?

You need look no further than your own home for the great education that your child deserves. Don't settle for a love that isn't true – love should have no strings attached!

Afterword

# Who is Lee Binz and What Can She Do for Me?

Number one best-selling homeschool author, Lee Binz is The HomeScholar. Her mission is "helping parents homeschool high school." Lee and her husband, Matt, homeschooled their two boys, Kevin and Alex, from elementary through High School.

Upon graduation, both boys received four-year, full tuition scholarships from their first choice university. This enables Lee to pursue her dream job - helping parents homeschool their children through high school.

On The HomeScholar website, you will find great products for creating homeschool transcripts and comprehensive records to help you amaze and impress colleges.

Find out why Andrew Pudewa, Director at Institute for Excellence in Writing says, "Lee Binz knows how to navigate this often confusing and frustrating labyrinth better than anyone."

You can find Lee online at:

HomeHighSchoolHelp.com

**If this book has been helpful, could you please take a minute to write us a quick review on Amazon?**

**Thank you!**

# Testimonials

## Thank You for Your Words of Wisdom

"This information is so much more than I ever could have hoped for from anyone! You're truly providing a wonderful service. Thank you so much for your help. Thank you for your words of wisdom. I will think up some other things to ask, I am sure. But for now, just know you've helped yet another 'worry wart' mom!!"

~Jennifer in Florida

----------

# Very Professional and Detailed

"Dear Lee,

I don't know how you could improve on what you already do and what you already offer. Thank you for helping me with my daughter that we just graduated. I worried about many things and when she started college I realized all my fears were unsubstantiated. Her college grades backed up the grades I gave her in high school. I could not have done it without you. Besides all your practical resources what really got me through was your encouragement. You helped me believe in myself and remember that the Lord wanted this for my daughter more than I did. Thank you from the bottom of my heart.

P.S. I still have 3 kids to graduate."

~ Mayra on Facebook

If you would like to get this type of support while homeschooling high school, learn about my **Gold Care Club** here:

GoldCareClub.com

# Also From
# The HomeScholar ...

- The HomeScholar Guide to College Admission and Scholarships: Homeschool Secrets to Getting Ready, Getting In and Getting Paid (Book and Kindle Book)
- Setting the Records Straight—How to Craft Homeschool Transcripts and Course Descriptions for College Admission and Scholarships (Book and Kindle Book)
- TechnoLogic: How to Set Logical Technology Boundaries and Stop the Zombie Apocalypse
- Finding the Faith to Homeschool High School
- The Easy Truth About Homeschool Transcripts (Kindle Book)
- Parent Training A la Carte (Online Training)

- Total Transcript Solution (Online Training, Tools and Templates)
- Comprehensive Record Solution (Online Training, Tools and Templates)
- Gold Care Club (Comprehensive Online Support and Training)
- Silver Training Club (Online Training)

## The HomeScholar Coffee Break Books Released or Coming Soon on Kindle and Paperback:

- Delight Directed Learning: Guiding Your Homeschooler Toward Passionate Learning
- Creating Transcripts for Your Unique Child: Help Your Homeschool Graduate Stand Out from the Crowd
- Beyond Academics: Preparation for College and for Life
- Planning High School Courses: Charting the Course Toward High School Graduation
- Graduate Your Homeschooler in Style: Make Your Homeschool Graduation Memorable
- Keys to High School Success: Get Your Homeschool High School Started Right!

- Getting the Most Out of Your Homeschool This Summer: Learning just for the Fun of it!
- Finding a College: A Homeschooler's Guide to Finding a Perfect Fit
- College Scholarships for High School Credit: Learn and Earn With This Two-for-One Strategy!
- College Admission Policies Demystified: Understanding Homeschool Requirements for Getting In
- A Higher Calling: Homeschooling High School for Harried Husbands (by Matt Binz, Mr. HomeScholar)
- Gifted Education Strategies for Every Child: Homeschool Secrets for Success
- College Application Essays: A Primer for Parents
- Creating Homeschool Balance: Find Harmony Between Type A and Type Zzz...
- Homeschooling the Holidays: Sanity Saving Strategies and Gift Giving Ideas
- Your Goals this Year: A Year by Year Guide to Homeschooling High School
- Making the Grades: A Grouch-Free Guide to Homeschool Grading
- High School Testing: Knowledge That Saves Money

- Getting the BIG Scholarships: Learn Expert Secrets for Winning College Cash!
- Easy English for Simple Homeschooling: How to Teach, Assess and Document High School English
- Scheduling—The Secret to Homeschool Sanity: Plan You Way Back to Mental Health
- Junior Year is the Key to High School Success: How to Unlock the Gate to Graduation and Beyond
- Upper Echelon Education: How to Gain Admission to Elite Universities
- How to Homeschool College: Save Time, Reduce Stress and Eliminate Debt
- Homeschool Curriculum That's Effective and Fun: Avoid the Crummy Curriculum Hall of Shame!
- Comprehensive Homeschool Records: Put Your Best Foot Forward to Win College Admission and Scholarships
- Options After High School: Steps to Success for College or Career
- How to Homeschool 9th and 10th Grade: Simple Steps for Starting Strong!

- Senior Year Step-by-Stcp: Simple Instructions for Busy Homeschool Parents
- How to Homeschool Independently: Do-it-Yourself Secrets to Rekindle the Love of Learning
- High School Math The Easy Way: Simple Strategies for Homeschool Parents in Over Their Heads
- Homeschooling Middle School with Powerful Purpose: How to Successfully Navigate 6th through 8th Grade
- Simple Science for Homeschooling High School: Because Teaching Science isn't Rocket Science!

Would you like to be notified when we offer the next *Coffee Break Books* for FREE during our Kindle promotion days? If so, leave your name and email below and we will send you a reminder.

HomeHighSchoolHelp.com/ freekindlebook

**Visit my Amazon Author Page!**

amazon.com/author/leebinz

Made in the USA
Middletown, DE
05 June 2018